THE STORY OF BANKSIDE

From the River Thames to St. George's Circus

London Borough of Southwark
Neighbourhood Histories No. 8

Southwark Cathedral and Old London Bridge
Based on Visscher's View, published 1616.

Front cover illustration:
Bankside, Southwark
After Hollar's View, published 1647.

ISBN 0 905849 07 8

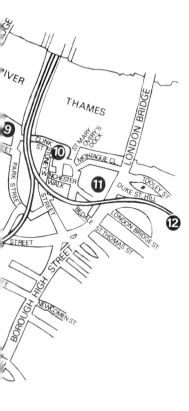

KEY TO MAP

1 Old Bargehouse Alley
2 Oxo Tower
3 King's Reach
4 Bankside Gallery
5 Bankside Power Station
6 Cardinal's Wharf and Cardinal Cap Alley
7 Bear Gardens Museum
8 Shakespeare Memorial; site of Globe and later of Courage's Factory
9 Anchor Pub
10 Remains of Winchester Palace
11 Southwark Cathedral
12 London Bridge Station
13 London Nautical School and portico of former Unitarian Church
14 United Africa House, site of the Rotunda
15 Christchurch
16 Hopton's Almshouses
17 Orbit House, site of Surrey Chapel, later "The Ring"
18 Blackfriars Settlement
19 Borough Community Centre, former Southwark Bridge Road Library
20 Fire Station
21 St. Saviour's and St. Joseph's Schools
22 Grotto Place Playground, site of Finch's Grotto
23 Friars School
24 Borough Underground Station
25 Site of Surrey Theatre
26 Royal Eye Hospital
27 Borough Road Library
28 St. George's Cathedral
29 St. George's School
30 Polytechnic of South Bank
31 The Obelisk
32 Imperial War Museum, former Bethlem Hospital
33 Notre Dame Convent and School
34 St. Jude's School
35 Charlotte Sharman School

Jnance Survey Map
f the Controller of
onery Office
HT RESERVED

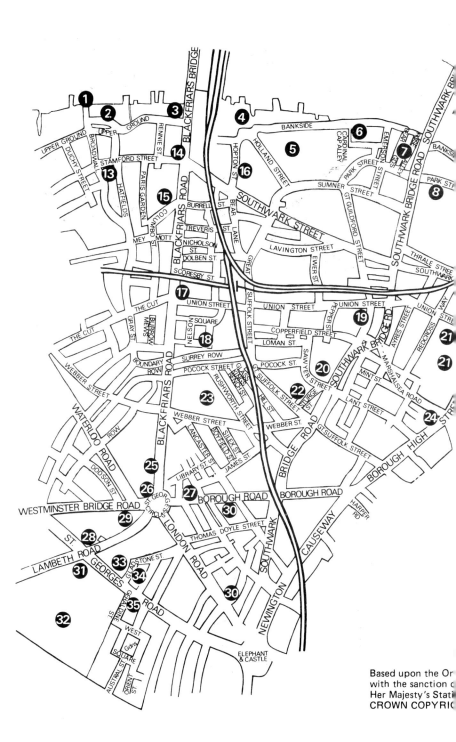

BLACKFRIARS BRIDGE

UPPER GROUND
DUCHY STREET
BROADWALL
UPPER GROUND
RENNIE ST.
STAMFORD STREET
HATFIELDS
PARIS GARDEN
MEY
COBURG
BLACKFRIARS ROAD
BURRELL ST.
TREVERIS
NICHOLSON ST.
DOLBEN ST.
SCORESBY ST.
BEAR LANE
BANKSIDE
CARDINAL CAP ALLEY
EMERSON
SOUTHWARK BRIDGE ROAD
BANKSIDE
PARK ST.
HOPTON ST.
HOLLAND STREET
SUMNER
PARK STREET
GT GUILDFORD STREET
SOUTHWARK STREET
LAVINGTON STREET
EWER ST.
GREAT
SUFFOLK STREET
THRALE STREET
SOUTHWARK

THE CUT
GRAY ST.
THE CUT
BURROW MEWS
WEBBER STREET
NELSON SQUARE
SURREY ROW
BOUNDARY ROW
POCOCK STREET
RUSHWORTH STREET
UNION STREET
UNION STREET
COPPERFIELD STREET
LOMAN ST.
PEPPER ST.
UNION STREET
POCOCK ST.
SAWYER STREET
AYRES STREET
REDCROSS WAY
UNION STREET

WATERLOO ROAD
ROW
DODSON ST.
WEBBER STREET
LANCASTER ST.
BOTFIELDS ST.
SILEX ST.
LIBRARY ST
JAMES ST.
GLASSHILL ST.
HILL ST.
WEBBER ST.
SUFFOLK STREET
LANT STREET
MINT ST.
MARSHALSEA ROAD
BOROUGH HIGH STREET

WESTMINSTER BRIDGE ROAD
GEORGE'S CIRCUS
LONDON ROAD
BOROUGH ROAD
BOROUGH ROAD
BRIDGE ROAD
HARPER RD.

ST.
LAMBETH ROAD
GEORGES ROAD
GLADSTONE ST.
THOMAS DOYLE STREET
SOUTHWARK
NEWINGTON
CAUSEWAY

GERALDINE ST.
WEST SQUARE
AUSTRAL ST.
OSWIN ST.
ELEPHANT & CASTLE

Based upon the Or
with the sanction c
Her Majesty's Stati
CROWN COPYRIC

2

THE STORY OF BANKSIDE

This booklet is a brief, simple introduction to the history of one part of the London Borough of Southwark. It is written mainly for young readers who live, or go to school in, or visit, that part of Southwark which stretches from London Bridge to west of Blackfriars Bridge and south as far as St. George's Circus. It overlaps with *Neighbourhood Histories No. 7; The Story of the Borough.*

Some suggestions for further reading are given at the end of each chapter, most of which are available at, or through, any Southwark library. Anyone wishing to make a more detailed study should visit the Southwark Local Studies Library, 211 Borough High Street, London SE1. Tel. 403 3507. This has a comprehensive collection of books, maps, illustrations, press-cuttings, microfilms and archives covering all parts of the London Borough of Southwark. The opening hours may be obtained from any library. An appointment in advance is helpful, and is essential for consultation of the archives, use of a microfilm reader, or for school party visits.

49 Bankside and Cardinal Cap Alley.

1. ON LONDON BRIDGE

Stand on London Bridge and look up river. The south bank as far as Blackfriars Bridge and just beyond, is the Southwark river-front. Today, apart from Southwark Cathedral, it is mainly a mixture of Victorian warehouses, modern office blocks, buildings under construction and some new open spaces. London Bridge, Southwark Bridge, Blackfriars Bridge and also railway bridges link it with the City and the north bank.

Now try to imagine the scene 2,000 or more years ago. There were no bridges then, probably no buildings, and no embankment. The muddy riverside was flooded at high tides. The only islands of firmer or higher ground were about where Borough High Street now approaches London Bridge. There was also rising ground across the river and the Romans saw that this was a good place for a crossing. On the north bank they built their city of Londinium. The Roman bridge was a little way down river from the modern bridge; its northern end was at Billingsgate. Borough High Street follows approximately the Roman road leading to this river crossing and Southwark, though not yet known by this name, became what it has remained ever since, the bridgehead or gateway to the City of London.

Archaeologists have found much evidence of the large Roman suburb which grew up around the bridgehead. Inside Southwark Cathedral you can walk on a piece of Roman pavement found in the Cathedral grounds. Roman sculptures were discovered hidden in a Roman well beneath the crypt. Part of a Roman road which led probably from the bridge to a ferry or ford at Lambeth was found below Montague Close, north of the Cathedral. West of it, on the site of Winchester Square, there were extensive Roman buildings with painted wall plaster and underfloor heating and others have been discovered on the former Courage's site in Park St.

After the Romans left, London Bridge was broken down by flood or fire and rebuilt several times in wood. According to a Norse saga, one exciting demolition took place in 1014 when Ethelred, King of England, with his ally Olaf (or Olave), King of Norway, sailed up the Thames to attack the Danes who had occupied the City and built fortifications in Southwark. The Danes were on the bridge, hurtling down stones and weapons, making advance impossible. Then Olaf thought of a plan. He made roofs for his ships with wood from old houses and stealthily his men rowed under the bridge, tied ropes to the piers which supported it, rowed hard down river and pulled down the bridge with the Danes on it, and thus recaptured London. A very old version of the rhyme, *London Bridge is Falling Down* tells the story —

> London Bridge is broken down
> Gold is won and bright renown
> Shields resounding
> War-horns sounding

> — — — — —

> Odin makes our Olaf win.

From *The Olaf Sagas.*

Until 1928 there was a St. Olave's Church near London Bridge. Over the centuries 'St. Olave's Street' became Tooley Street.

The most famous bridge linking Southwark with the City was Old London Bridge. This magnificent stone bridge was the work of the Bridgemaster, Peter de Colechurch, and took over thirty years to build, from 1176 – 1209. Houses, shops and a chapel were built on it and at the Southwark end was the Great Stone Gate. It was in use for over 600 years. Kings entered London in state, rebels attacked, and all the crowds or ordinary travellers and merchants entered and left London by this bridge as, until 1750, it was the only bridge over the Thames in the London area. The building of other bridges and the rebuilding twice of London Bridge will be the subject of a later chapter.

Finding out more

1 There are many good books on Old London Bridge, e.g. *London Bridge* by P. Jackson (told mainly in pictures) and *Old London Bridge* by G. Home, Chaps. 1 & 2.

2 For Roman Southwark see also *Neighbourhood Histories No. 7.*

3 See finds from Roman Southwark in the Cuming Museum, Walworth Road, SE17, and a model of the Roman bridge in the Museum of London.

4 Read *Rescuing the Past in Southwark* publ. by Southwark and Lambeth Archaeological Excavation Committee, 1984.

2. SOUTHWARK CATHEDRAL

The oldest building in Southwark, and one of the oldest in London, is the church next to London Bridge which is now Southwark Cathedral. There has been a church on this site for over 1,000 years. Although there have been many changes you can easily recognise the building on the oldest pictures of Southwark, such as the panorama printed in 1616 by Visscher. The bells rang in 1577 when Queen Elizabeth I attended a wedding at nearby Winchester Palace. Recast, they still ring out above the noise of modern traffic.

Old legends say the first church was founded by Mary, daughter of John Overs, the ferryman who rowed people across the river. Other stories say it was built, or rebuilt, by St. Swithun, Bishop of Winchester 852-862 A.D. Certainly there was a 'monasterium', a 'minster' or large church, here in the time of William the Conqueror, as it is mentioned in Domesday Book in 1086. It was rebuilt about 1106 and again a century later after a fire. The tower was completed in 1520. In the Middle Ages it was known as the Priory of St. Mary Overie, 'over the river' and belonged to the Augustinian Canons, black-robed priest monks, who lived in buildings round the cloisters to the north of the church. At the Reformation, when Henry VIII dissolved the monasteries, the priory church became the parish church of St. Saviour. The cloisters passed to the father of Lord Montague. The site is still called Montague Close.

The church survived many troubles. For a time the beautiful retro-choir or Lady Chapel, behind the high altar, was actually let to a baker, who kept pigs there. About 200 years later the wooden roof was taken down and the nave fell into ruins. Some called the church 'St. Saviour's Folly' and said it should be pulled down. A chapel at the east end was actually demolished in 1830 during the rebuilding of London Bridge. Fortunately the architect, George Gwilt, insisted that the church itself should be preserved and it was he who beautifully restored the retro-choir. In 1897 a new nave was built. In 1905 St. Saviour's became the Cathedral for the new diocese of Southwark, which stretches from Richmond to Woolwich and as far south as Reigate.

Go inside and take in the beauty and peace of the building. Looking round you find clues to every stage in the Cathedral's history. In the north aisle are two rounded Norman arches which survived the fire of 1213. The east end, the choir and the retro-choir with its lovely columns, date from the 13th and 14th centuries. The nave was rebuilt copying this Early English style of architecture.

The rebuilt nave has a stone roof. Some of the carved 'bosses' which decorated the old wooden roof are now on show at the back of the church. The 15th century woodcarvers must have had a lively imagination. Notice especially the head of the Devil eating up Judas Iscariot and the faces showing various vices, the fat face for gluttony, or greediness, and the twisted tongue of the liar. Some bosses have been placed on the tower ceiling in the centre of the church, which has been cleaned and newly gilded.

The carved stone screen behind the high altar was presented about 1520 by Richard Fox, Bishop of Winchester. The figures on it are modern but represent people connected with Southwark history, for example, St. Olave, Bishop Fox and King Edward VII who attended the service when the church became a cathedral. Above the altar is the east window where the morning sun shines through a stained glass picture of 'The Lord in Glory' by the 20th century artist Ninian Comper. At the west end of the Cathedral is a modern bronze sculpture of the Holy Family.

The Cathedral is the work of many hands and many centuries. In it are also memorials to many people who have lived in Southwark and worshipped here. In the north choir aisle is a lifelike figure of a knight in armour, one of the oldest wooden figures in England. Perhaps he was a member of the great Warenne family, the Earls of Surrey, the county of which Southwark was then a part. Near him is John Gower, poet and friend of Chaucer. During his last years he lived in the precincts of St. Mary Overie Priory. His head is resting on the three books he wrote, one in English, one in French and one in Latin. As you can see from their dress, Alderman Richard Humble and John Trehearne lived in the time of Shakespeare. On the other side of the Cathedral is a memorial to Shakespeare himself, erected in 1912. A later chapter will show why there is this memorial in Southwark and why Shakespeare lovers from all over the world visit the Cathedral and nearby Bankside.

The Harvard Chapel restored 'by the sons and friends of Harvard

University' commemorates John Harvard who was christened in St. Saviour's Church and lived in Southwark until he emigrated to America. By his will he helped to establish the college which became one of the great universities of the U.S.A.

Finding out more

1 Good guide books are on sale in the Cathedral including, for young people, *Look at Southwark Cathedral.*

2 Read *Southwark story* by F. Higham, also many books and articles in the Local Studies Library.

3 Read *Buildings of England: London 2: South* by B. Cherry and N. Pevsner 1983. P. 564-72.

4 For John Harvard, see *Neighbourhood Histories No. 7.*

5 The Cuming Museum has sculpture from St. Mary Overie and models of Southwark Cathedral.

3. WINCHESTER PALACE AND PARIS GARDEN

Centuries ago, when Southwark Cathedral was still the Priory of St. Mary Overie, its neighbours were fine mansions with gardens and meadows stretching down to the river. In Clink Street you will find all that remains standing of any of these buildings, the west wall and other traces of the Great Hall of Winchester Palace, the London residence from about 1107 – 1626 of the Bishop of Winchester. High up in the wall is the beautiful stone tracery of a 14th century rose window. Winchester Square was once the inner courtyard of the palace.

The name Park Street reminds you of the Bishop of Winchester's park, or estate, which stretched from the priory walls, in what is now Cathedral Street, to Gravel Lane, now renamed Great Suffolk Street. A document described it as 'all the episcopal pastures belonging to the bishop's manor in Southwark'. There were sheep and cows, ponds, or 'pike gardens', constructed to supply the bishop's household with fish, a granary for storing corn and a mill. In those days there were many water mills along the Southwark riverside to grind the corn brought up river by ship.

Bishops were often great statesmen as well as churchmen. From river stairs at the end of Stoney Street the bishop could go by boat to the king's court at Westminster. In 1424, when Cardinal Beaufort was Bishop of Winchester, his niece Joan was married to King James I of Scotland in St. Mary Overie's church and the wedding feast was held in the Great Hall. You can see the red cardinal's hat and coat of arms of Bishop Beaufort in the south transept of Southwark Cathedral, the part of the church which he rebuilt after a fire. The last bishop to live at Winchester Palace was the saintly Lancelot Andrewes, who died in 1626. There is a lifelike figure of him on his tomb in the Cathedral. He

Winchester Palace, 1828.

was one of the scholars who prepared the Authorised Version of the Bible, the translation used in most English churches until recent years.

During the Civil War, Winchester Palace was used by Parliament as a prison for their Royalist captives. Afterwards it was divided up and let for housing and industry, until 1814, when most of it was destroyed by a fire. What survived was built into new warehouses and it was only when these were demolished that the rose window was again revealed to view.

When the bishop lived at Winchester Palace other great churchmen also had riverside estates, for example, the Bishop of Rochester's estate on the site of Borough Market, and, east of London Bridge, the 'inns' or London residences of the Prior of Lewes, the Abbot of St. Augustine's, Canterbury, and the Abbot of Battle in Sussex. Today only the Archbishop of Canterbury still has Lambeth Palace as his London home.

The next estate up river from the Bishop of Winchester was the Manor of Paris Garden, named probably after Robert de Paris, who had a house there in the time of Richard II. A stream flowing beside Gravel Lane led to Paris Garden Stairs, a millpond and the Pudding Mill. For about 200 years this Manor was held by the Knights Templars. Marble figures of these crusader knights lie in their Temple Church across the river.

To protect their lands against flooding the occupants of these riverside estates built a river wall. Raised in recent years, it continued to prevent North Southwark from being flooded at extra high tides until the risk was finally removed by the completion of the Thames barrier in 1984. Bankside is the road along the river wall of the Bishop of Winchester's estate. 'The Banck' is marked on the earliest printed map of London, the 'Agas' map of 1560. The continuation of Bankside is Upper Ground, the river wall of Paris Garden. In fact this manor was surrounded by walls and ditches. Its western boundary is still called Broadwall.

In 1671 a church was built in Paris Garden and the neighbourhood became the Parish of Christ Church. Behind the rebuilt Christ Church, Blackfriars Road, is a little street, once the main street of the parish, which has been renamed Paris Garden.

Finding out more

1 Read *Survey* Vol. XXII Chaps 6 & 18.

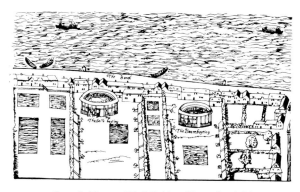

Bear-Baiting and Bull-Baiting Rings, Bankside
After the "Agas" map, c. 1560.

2 Study *The A to Z of Elizabethan London* (the 'Agas' map) and *The A to Z of Georgian London* (Rocque's map of 1746). London Topographical Society publs.

3 Read *Old Bankside* by G. Golden, publ. 1951, Chap 3.

4 Read *An historical account of the Parish of Christ Church* by W. J. Meymott.

4. IN CLINK

Everyone must know what it means to be 'in clink'. Fewer know that the prison which probably gave its name to all others was the Clink in Clink Street on the Bishop of Winchester's estate. In the Middle Ages the estate was a 'liberty', outside the power of the City or other authorities. The bishop had his own court to try offenders. Punishments included a whipping-post, stocks and, for women, a cucking or ducking-stool, for ducking them in the sewer at Bank End. Worst punishment of all was the bishop's prison, the notorious Clink, just west of the Great Hall of Winchester Palace. All prisons were horrible in those days, but the Clink was especially nasty because it was low-lying, partly an underground dungeon, and very damp, being between the river, the common sewer and the pike gardens. How it got its name is uncertain. Probably it was from an old word for a lock-up, similar to clench, as when you clench, or shut tight your fists, or your teeth.

John Stow, the historian of London, writing in 1598, said the Clink was 'a prison for such as should brabble or frey, or break the peace on the Bank'. Sadly it was not only used for wrong-doers. People whose religious beliefs differed from those in power also suffered. During Queen Mary's reign when Stephen Gardiner was Bishop of Winchester, Protestants such as John Hooper, Bishop of Gloucester and John Rogers, who published an English version of the Bible, were tried in St. Mary Overie, imprisoned in the Clink, and then led by night across Old London Bridge to be burnt at the stake at Smithfield. In Queen Elizabeth's time and after, it was the Roman Catholics' turn to be imprisoned and in some cases, sent to be hanged. A priest, John Gerard, actually said he 'preferred the Clink to other prisons on account of the great number of Catholics I found there. Instead of lewd songs and blasphemies, prayers met my ears'. John Gerard House, Union Street, is named after him. Protestant 'Separatists', Henry Barrowe and John Greenwood, were also put in the Clink, where they spent their time writing books. They were hanged at Tyburn, but their ideas inspired the Pilgrim Fathers, when, in 1620, they sailed for America seeking freedom of worship. In its later years the Clink was moved to another building and used mainly for people who got into debt. It was finally destroyed in 1780.

Though the prison is happily a thing of the past, you are still reminded that this neighbourhood was once 'the Liberty of the Clink'. Many little streets have bollards, iron posts put up to prevent carts mounting the pavements, which have the inscription 'Clink 1812', the date they were bought by the Commissioners for Clink Pavements at two guineas (£2.10) each from Samuel Bishop's Iron & Nail Warehouse, 8 Bankside. This was during the wars against Napoleon and they are cast like the barrel of a gun with a cannon ball in its mouth. Real old guns were used in some cases for this purpose. Similar bollards in Cathedral Street were erected by the Wardens of St. Saviour's.

Finding out more

1 Read *Survey* Vol. XXII, p. 55-56.

2 Read *Old Southwark* by W. Rendle, p. 196-223.

3 Read *Mayflower & Pilgrim Story,* L.B. Southwark publ., Chap. 3.

5. ENTERTAINMENTS OF OLD BANKSIDE

For citizens of London in olden days the place to come for entertainments was Bankside. It was easy to reach across Old London Bridge, or by ferryboat landing at one of the many riverside stairs, for example St. Mary Overie's Stairs leading to Stoney Street, Bank End Stairs opposite what is now the Anchor, or Paris Garden Stairs. Most have gone but west of Blackfriars Bridge you can still find Old Barge House Alley, where the royal barge was kept, leading to Old Barge House Stairs.

Many inns welcomed visitors to Bankside. One was the Cardinal's Cap, named perhaps after Cardinal Wolsey who was Bishop of Winchester 1529-30. Actors at the Bankside theatres used to meet here. Narrow Cardinal Cap Alley led to the inn. Cardinal's Wharf, No. 49 Bankside, which took its place, was built about 1700. Falcon Point, a block of flats near Blackfriars Bridge, is named after the Falcon, a large riverside inn with twenty-nine rooms for travellers and a stable for their horses. Many ferry boats landed at Falcon Stairs. On 23rd February 1668, Samuel Pepys wrote in his famous diary: 'Lord's Day (Sunday) by water over to Southwark and so walked to the Falcon on Bankside, there got another boat and so to Westminster'. On 6th September 1666, from 'a little alehouse on the Bankside' Pepys watched the Great Fire of London. The only old inn still standing is the Anchor which was built about 1775 on the site of a much older inn called the Castle on the Hoop.

Many of the entertainments of old Bankside were of a kind that the City did not want within its walls. Men came here to find their pleasure and spend their money on the women of the 'stews'. This was an old word for fishponds and the houses of ill repute may have got their name from the nearby pike gardens. There was much gambling, even on the bowling matches played in the alleys off Bankside, particularly Horseshoe Alley. According to a writer of the time 'A bowl-alley is the place where there are three things thrown away besides bowls, to wit, time, money and curses'.

The alley still called Bear Gardens reminds you of the cruel sports of bear and bull baiting for which Bankside was especially famous. Halfway down the alley, where it widens out, and where the Bear Gardens Museum now stands, you are on the site of the last of the bear-baiting rings. The sport consisted of putting a bear in the ring to fight with a dog. Crowds watched from the stands, betting on which animal would win. As a poet wrote in 1550,

> 'What folly is this to keep with danger
> A great mastiff dog and a foul ugly bear,
> And to this only end, to see them two fight
> With a terrible tearing, a full ugly sight;
> And yet methink those men be most fools of all
> Whose store of money is but very small
> And yet every Sunday they will surely spend
> One penny or two, the bearward's (bearkeeper's)
>   living to mend,
> At Paris Garden each Sunday, a man shall not fail
> To find two or three hundred, for the bearward's vaile
>   (benefit).'

> *Of Bearbaiting* by Robert Crowley (spelling modernised)

Queen Elizabeth I brought the French Ambassador, by barge, to watch the bear-baiting. In 1604 Edward Alleyn, who later founded Dulwich College, obtained the title of Master of the Royal Bears, Bulls and Mastiff dogs. When Pepys and his wife visited the Bear Garden they saw 'some good sport of the bulls tossing of the dogs; one into the very boxes', but that other famous diarist, John Evelyn, came away from a visit in 1670 'heartily weary of the rude and dirty pastime'. In 1682 the last Bear Garden was finally closed and demolished.

If you could have visited old Bankside you would have found it noisy, exciting and lively but also rather a nasty place. Its entertainments attracted the riff-raff of London. The smell of the open ditches, used as sewers, the bear pits, dog-kennels and offal dumped by the butchers of London to feed the animals, and also the crowds of unwashed spectators, would have hit you when you landed from the ferry. No wonder outbreaks of plague were especially deadly here.

Yet this neighbourhood had its hour of glory. People all over the world have heard of Bankside, Southwark, because of one short period in its history, the age of Shakespeare, the golden age of English drama, when it was the theatreland of Elizabethan London.

Finding out more

1 Read *Survey* Vol XXII, p. 66-71.

2 Read *Old Bankside,* Chap. X.

3 Study *Bankside Broadsheets* by G. Golden, (single page notes and drawings).

6. SHAKESPEARE AND THE GLOBE

Like other entertainments which attracted crowds, theatres and actors were not popular with the City authorities. It was, therefore, on Bankside, Southwark, outside the City's jurisdiction, that some of the first theatres in England were built. There were no less than four Bankside theatres, the Rose, the Swan, the Hope and, 'the glory of the Bank', Shakespeare's own theatre, the Globe.

At these theatres the audiences saw for the first time many of the finest plays in the English language, the works of Shakespeare and those of other great playwrights. Shakespeare's early plays were produced at the Rose which was noted also for works by Christopher Marlowe, for example, *Dr. Faustus,* the story of a man who sold his soul to the devil. Edward Alleyn was the leading actor and the manager was Philip Henslowe. Ben Johnson's famous comedy *Bartholomew Fair* was performed at the Hope, a theatre built in 1614 by Alleyn and Henslowe, which was used also as a bear-baiting ring.

The Globe belonged to the group of actors known as the Lord Chamberlain's, or later as the King's Men, of whom Shakespeare was a member. He wrote his plays for them and sometimes also acted with them. The company, who had earlier acted together at the Theatre in Shoreditch, built in 1576, brought the Theatre, in pieces, across to Bankside where it was rebuilt and renamed and, in 1599, reopened, as the Globe. Richard Burbage was the leading actor. Shakespeare's plays produced here included *Henry V, Julius Caesar, Hamlet, Macbeth* and *Anthony and Cleopatra.*

Like all the theatres, the Globe was a round or polygonal building, a wooden 'O' with the centre open to the sky. Performances could only take place on fine days and by daylight. A flag flying on the turret showed that a play was to be performed and a trumpeter announced when it was about to begin. A drawing made by a Dutchman, Johannes de Witt, about 1596, of the interior of the Swan gives some idea of what it was probably like inside the Globe. Richer people sat in the covered galleries overlooking three sides of the stage. The gallery on the fourth side, behind the stage, was used by the musicians, or perhaps as a balcony for the love-scene in *Romeo and Juliet*. The 'groundlings' stood in the space around the 'apron stage'. There was little or no scenery, but with Shakespeare's words, the audiences could picture even the battlefield of Agincourt –

> . . . can this cockpit hold
> The vasty fields of France? Or may we cram
> Within this wooden O the very casques
> That did affright the air at Agincourt?
>
> Think when we talk of horses that you see them
> Printing their proud hoofs in the receiving earth
> For 'tis your thoughts that now must deck our kings.

Shakespeare: Henry V

Cannonballs were rolled in the turret to create the sound of thunder or were fired for battle and ceremonial scenes. In fact, this was how the first Globe was burnt down. In 1613 during a performance of Shakespeare's *Henry VIII,* cannon set fire to the thatched roof of the galleries. It was rebuilt with a tiled roof, but its great days were over. Like the other theatres, it closed at the outbreak of the Civil War and in 1644 was demolished. Later it was the West End that became London's theatreland.

The Shakespeare Memorial in Southwark Cathedral has a view in the background of the Globe and the Bankside that Shakespeare knew so well and where for a time he may have lived, within the Bishop of Winchester's Liberty. Above the memorial is a stained glass window with characters from his plays such as Bottom with the ass's head, fat Falstaff, Hamlet with a skull, and also the seven ages of man from *As you like it.* In the floor of the choir is a plaque telling you that

Shakespeare Memorial, Southwark Cathedral.

Shakespeare's brother Edmund, 'a player', was buried in the church. There are similar plaques with the names of John Fletcher and Philip Massinger, other playwrights of Shakespeare's day.

On Shakespeare's birthday, 23rd April, a memorial service is held and a Shakespeare Pilgrimage sets out from the Cathedral. You do not see much to remind you of Elizabethan Bankside, but you can discover among the warehouses and office blocks the approximate sites of the famous theatres. A plaque on the south side of Park Street reads 'Here stood the Globe Playhouse of Shakespeare'. Rose Alley which led to the Rose Theatre is still a turning off Park Street. The Hope was in Bear Gardens. The Swan, the largest of the theatres, was in Paris Garden about where Lloyds' Computer Centre is today.

Finding out more

1 Read *Survey* Vol. XXII, Chap. 8.

2 Read *Shakespeare's Theatre* by C. W. Hodges.

3 Read *Old Bankside* by G. Golden, Chaps. VIII & IX.

4 The Cuming Museum and Bear Gardens Museum have models of the Globe.

5 The Local Studies Library has a special collection on Shakespeare and the Bankside theatres.

7. CRAFTSMEN AND ARTISTS

Magnificent stained glass, marble monuments still to be seen in many churches, early printed books, pottery and glass for the table, all these were made in Southwark before, during, or soon after the days of Shakespeare. It was a noted place for skilled craftsmen. They had their workshops near the river so that ships could bring the raw materials and take away the finished products. The bumpy unmade-up roads of those days were used as little as possible; only to deliver goods by horse and cart from the ports to inland places. Many of the craftsmen were immigrants or religious refugees, mostly Dutch or 'Flemings' from what are now Holland and Belgium. They settled in Southwark to avoid the restrictions imposed by the City on newcomers who tried to set up in business.

Between 1515 and 1531 the 'Southwark School of Glaziers' who worked within the bounds of the old St. Thomas' Hospital in St. Thomas' Street, off Borough High Street, made the famous stained glass windows for King's College Chapel, Cambridge. In glorious colours, the windows illustrate the stories of the Bible. Three of the Southwark School, in turn, had the honour of being appointed as King's Glazier; Barnard Flower, Galyon Hone and Peter Nicholson, relative of James Nicholson, another of the glaziers. Their names are not so well known as Shakespeare's but their glass is one of the glories of England.

Some of the earliest English printers lived in Southwark, for example, Peter Treveris, who in 1527 printed in Southwark a large history book with woodcut illustrations entitled *Higden's Polychronicon.* The first complete Bible in English to be printed in England, a translation from the Latin by Miles Coverdale, has on its title-page 'Imprinted in Southwarke in Saint Thomas Hospitale by James Nycolson, 1537.' Nycolson (or Nicholson), earlier a glazier, had turned to printing. Throughout the centuries, printing and publishing have continued to be important North Southwark industries. Crane House, Lavington Street, is the headquarters of a printing firm, Lett's Diaries are produced in Borough Road and the headquarters of the International Publishing Corporation is in Stamford Street.

Now look again at the memorials in Southwark Cathedral and think of the sculptors who made these life-like figures. Many of them lived on the Southwark riverside where marble shipped from Italy and elsewhere could be landed for their work. Gheerart Jannson, a Dutchman, later known as Gerald Johnson, and his five sons, had a wharf just down river from London Bridge. One of them carved the figure of Lancelot Andrewes. Another made the monument of Shakespeare for his tomb at Stratford-on-Avon.

William Cure of Amsterdam and his family, who lived near old St. Thomas Hospital, made the memorial to Mary Queen of Scots, in Westminster Abbey and also that of Alderman Humble in Southwark Cathedral. Monuments such as these show how people looked and dressed four hundred years ago. In the north transept of Southwark Cathedral there are even farm-workers with rakes and pitchforks on a monument by Nicholas Stone, another of the Southwark sculptors.

Recent finds by archaeologists have shown that pottery, jugs, cups, dishes and cooking pots for London tables and kitchens were probably made on Bankside even in the Middle Ages. In the 17th and early 18th centuries Montague Close was one of the most important places for the manufacture of English delftware, tin-glaze pottery, mostly blue and white, similar to that made in Delft, Holland. In 1969 archaeologists dicovered three kilns where this pottery was made. Another of the riverside potteries was in the street still called Potters' Fields, off Tooley Street. Potters from Southwark founded factories in Lambeth, Bristol and Liverpool, the best known names in English delftware.

After St. Mary Overie Priory was dissolved, Winchester Palace abandoned, and the theatres and bear-gardens demolished, all this neighbourhood became a hive of industry. Some of the earliest workshops were 'glasshouses' producing bottles, drinking glasses and window glass. The Falcon Glassworks became especially famous after 1803 under the Apsley Pellatts who produced works of art such as beautiful cut-glass and coloured glass decorated with white cameos.

The phrase 'on tenterhooks' (as, for example, when you are waiting for exam results!) reminds you of another old Southwark industry. Weavers used long tenter-frames to stretch their cloth on tenterhooks to make it smooth and even. Rocques' Map of 1746 shows at least nine 'tenter grounds' in the Bankside neighbourhood.

Monument to Richard Humble, 1616,
in Southwark Cathedral.

Finding out more

1 Read *Old Southwark* by W. Rendle p. 130-4 and p. 262-6.

2 Read *Days in the Factories* by G. Dodd, 1843, Chaps. 12 and 15.

3 There are special articles on most industries in the Local Studies Library – e.g. *An illustrated guide to the windows of King's College Cambridge; The first printers in 16th century Southwark, 1514-40; Montague Close excavations* by G. J. Dawson; *London Potters c1570-1710* by R. Edwards; *'Embroyder'd Suits'* in *Friends of Southwark Cathedral* Record 1982; *Old London Glasshouses, 1. Southwark* by F. Buckley; *At the Sign of the Crane* by B. McConnell.

4 Delftware from Montagu Close is in the Cuming Museum.

5 Southwark delftware, model of a Southwark kiln and reconstruction of a clay pipe kiln found in Southwark are in the Museum of London.

8. THAMES BRIDGES

On a boat trip from Westminster to the Tower you pass under many bridges. It is difficult to imagine this stretch of the river when the only bridge was Old London Bridge. The first of the new bridges was Westminster, opened in 1750. The first to link Southwark with the City was Blackfriars Bridge, opened in 1769 and rebuilt a hundred years later. The original Southwark Bridge, built in 1819, was a good example of the use of cast-iron in bridge building. People paid a toll to go over it. In his novel *Little Dorrit,* Charles Dickens described John Chivery 'putting his penny on the toll plate of the iron bridge'. Southwark Bridge was rebuilt and reopened in 1921.

By the 19th century Old London Bridge itself, after 600 years, was in constant need of repair and it was decided to replace it. The design chosen for the new London Bridge was that of John Rennie, the great engineer who had already designed the first Southwark Bridge and the first Waterloo Bridge. His son Sir John Rennie, another celebrated engineer, supervised the rebuilding. The family lived in Stamford Street and had their engineering works in Hopton Street.

The new London Bridge was built 100 feet up river from the old, the line of Borough High Street being altered to lead to the new bridge. Old London Bridge was supported on nineteen stone arches which only left room for the smallest boats to get through, and so restricted the flow of the river that going under the bridge was a dangerous business, known as 'shooting the rapids'. Rennie's new bridge had only five arches and was also much wider than the old bridge. One remaining arch gives you an idea of what it looked like. It may be seen from Montague Close, carrying Borough High Street across Tooley Street, an early example of a flyover.

When Rennie's bridge was opened in 1831, there was only horse-drawn traffic, but it bore the weight of modern motor transport until replaced, on the same site, by the present London Bridge. This streamlined masterpiece of modern engineering, opened in 1973, was built under the direction of the City Engineer, Harold Knox-King, and consists of three parallel bridges of pre-stressed concrete linked together. It has only three arches and two piers and even these are not needed for its main support. When Rennie's bridge was taken down, the stones were numbered and it has been re-erected at Lake Havasu, Arizona, U.S.A.

Tower Bridge, linking Bermondsey with the City, was opened in 1894.

Other bridges carry railway lines across the river. From London Bridge Station trains run on a viaduct high above Borough High Street, Borough Market and Clink Street to Cannon Street Railway Bridge, built in 1866. From the Anchor you get a good view of this bridge. Other railway bridges across Borough High Street, Southwark Bridge Road and Blackfriars Road take the line from London Bridge to Waterloo and Charing Cross. From Blackfriars Bridge you can see the railway bridge which carries trains to Blackfriars Station.

Finding out more

1 There are many books on the bridges, e.g. *Thames Crossings,* by G. Phillips, 1981.

2 Do walks suggested in *Industrial Archaeology Walks in London No. 1 Southwark: Waterloo to London Bridge* and *No. 2 Blackfriars to Tower Bridge,* GLIAS (Greater London Industrial Archaeology Society) publs.

3 From plaques on London Bridge find out who opened it, names of builders and the boundary mark of St. Saviour's parish.

4 Railway bridges cross many North Southwark streets. Where do the trains go that cross your street?

5 Read *Charles Dickens and Southwark.* L.B. Southwark publ. Chaps. 2 & 8.

6   For Tower Bridge and for London Bridge Station see *Neighbourhood Histories No. 5.*

7   An 18th century alcove from Old London Bridge may be seen in Guy's Hospital courtyard and the coat-of-arms from the gateway has been set up over the King's Arms pub, Newcomen Street.

9. FIELDS TO STREETS

> 'St. George's Fields are fields no more,
> The trowel supersedes the plough;
> Swamps huge and inundate of yore,
> Are changed to civic villas now'.
>   *The Spread of London,* publ. 1813.

Before the Thames bridges were built, north Southwark, south of Bankside and west of Borough High Street, was nearly all open country. The ground was so marshy that the first Christ Church sank up to its windows within fifty years and had to be rebuilt. South of Paris Garden, or Christ Church parish, were St. George's Fields stretching as far as the Elephant and Castle. There were no main roads. Footpaths were sometimes impassable, as you can guess from their old names. Great Guildford Street was Bandy Leg Walk, part of Great Suffolk Street was Dirty Lane. Hopton Street, Colombo Street and Burrell Street were all part of the Green Walk.

In fine weather this was a pleasant neighbourhood for a day's outing from the crowded City streets. Gerarde's *Herbal,* published 1597, mentioned the water violets growing in the ditches of St. George's Fields. Where the Imperial War Museum now stands was the Dog and Duck, a refreshment house named after the sport of setting dogs to chase the ducks swimming on the three ponds which surrounded it. In 1730 the Dog & Duck became St. George's Spa, where ladies and gentlemen came to 'take the waters' for their health, or to bathe in them, and also to listen to music and play bowls or skittles. Grotto Place playground, near Southwark Bridge Road, marks the site of Finch's Grotto Gardens. The grotto and a fountain were built by Thomas Finch in 1760 over another spring which was said to have medicinal value.

St. George's Fields were also used for archery practice and when England was at war, soldiers trained here. Rebels and rioters might gather in these fields. In 1780, thousands of Protestants who disagreed with an Act giving more freedom to Roman Catholics, paraded under their leader, Lord George Gordon, before marching to parliament to present their petition. On the way the Gordon Rioters burned down the Clink and also the King's Bench Prison in Borough Road.

Large-scale development in St. George's Fields began when the new bridges were built. These bridges would have been useless without good roads leading to them and the whole pattern of main roads which you see on a modern map was laid out at this time. It was a good early example of town-planning. St. George's Circus was planned as a circular junction where the roads met. The Duke of Clarence pub on the corner of London Road and Borough Road still has a concave front showing it was part of this circle.

The roads from St. George's Circus, leading to the bridges, are Blackfriars Road, Waterloo Road, Westminster Bridge Road and Lambeth Road. Borough Road links with Southwark Bridge Road and Borough High Street. Roads leading south are London Road and St. George's Road. The Cut was cut through open fields to link Blackfriars Road and Westminster Bridge Road.

The Obelisk, St. George's Road.

The Obelisk, now in the grounds of the Imperial War Museum, was an important early road sign. From 1771 until 1905 it stood in the centre of St. George's Circus. Travellers could find the direction and distance from Westminster, Fleet Street and London Bridge inscribed on three of its sides. The south side says it was erected in the reign of George III, when Brass Crosby was Lord Mayor. Originally the Obelisk had lights hanging from each corner so that it could be seen and read at night.

When new roads opened up St. George's Fields, many charitable institutions bought land and erected fine buildings here. One was the School for the Indigent Blind, the first school in London for blind children, at the junction of Lambeth Road and London Road. Another was the Philanthropic Society's School in St. George's Road which provided for homeless children whose parents were in prison and who might become thieves themselves in order to live.

The only one of these buildings left standing is now used as the Imperial War Museum. It was erected, not as a museum, but as the Bethlem Hospital for mental patients, which moved here from the City in 1815. Its spacious buildings and large grounds show that people were already beginning to realise that mentally ill people should be treated with kindness and not just regarded as 'lunatics'. James Lewis, the hospital surveyor, drew the plans, including the magnificent entrance with its columns and pediment, rather like a Greek temple. The copper-covered dome was added in 1844. In 1926, when the hospital moved to Beckenham, the grounds became the Geraldine Mary Harmsworth Park, named after the mother of Viscount Rothermere, who had bought the land and presented it to the London County Council. The side wings of the old hospital were demolished but in 1936 the central section became the Imperial War Museum.

As well as these important buildings, houses and shops began to appear along all the main roads, and many smaller ones, and soon, instead of fields, the whole of this area became a maze of streets.

Finding out more

1 Read the *Survey* Vol. XXV, Chaps. 5, 6, 7 & 9.

2 Study *Scenes from the Past* Ser. 2, No. 2. L.B. Southwark publ.

3 How far was the Obelisk from Westminster Hall and London Bridge?

4 See the Dog and Duck sign in the Cuming Museum.

5 Visit the Imperial War Museum.

The Ring, Blackfriars Road, c. 1920's.

10. CIRCUSES, THEATRES AND MUSIC HALLS

New bridges and roads made it easier for people to come out to the neighbourhood around Blackfriars Road and St. George's Circus. It became a place to find entertainment, as Bankside had been two hundred years earlier.

First there were the circuses. There had been nothing like them since the days of ancient Rome. Astleys, Westminster Bridge Road, Lambeth, was the earliest, opened in 1770 by a marvellous horseman, Philip Astley. In 1782 Charles Hughes, one of Astley's horsemen, and Charles Dibden, song-writer, opened the Royal Circus in Blackfriars Road, near the Obelisk. It was easily seen from a distance with its figure of the winged horse, Pegasus, on the roof.

In 1809 the Royal Circus, rebuilt after a fire, was converted into the famous Surrey Theatre. It made its name in the early years with one play, *Black-eyed Susan,* which ran for 400 nights. A popular actor, T. P. Cooke played the sailor hero. Later, when George Conquest, and afterwards his son, were managers, children especially loved its marvellous Christmas pantomimes, with scenes such as 'Davey Jones Locker', described in a playbill as a 'transcendentally grand transformation scene, refulgent temples of bright water, Neptune's homage to Britannia'. At other times, there were thrilling melodramas or scenes from Shakespeare or from Dickens' novels such as *Oliver Twist*. The 'Surrey' was not finally demolished until 1934.

Nearer to Blackfriars Bridge there were two large round buildings. On the west side of the road was the Rotunda, built in 1788 for the Leverian Museum, an early Natural History Museum, with stuffed animals and birds from all over the world and objects brought home by Captain Cook. When the collection was sold in 1806 some items were bought by Richard Cuming of Walworth and are now in the Cuming Museum. The Rotunda was then occupied for a time by the Surrey Institution, a learned society, and later was used for circuses, plays, concerts, and meetings.

'The Ring' at the corner of Blackfriars Road and Union Street is well remembered by older people as a popular attraction of a different kind. In its later years it was a boxing ring. The building had been erected, originally, in 1782, as the Surrey Chapel, for the famous preacher Rowland Hill. People said it was round, or octagonal in shape so that the devil had no corners to hide in! After World War II, United Africa House was built on the site of the Rotunda and Orbit House on the site of the Ring.

The earliest Victorian music-halls were in north Southwark and Lambeth. This kind of entertainment began in halls attached to public houses, where people could sit and drink and join in the songs. The Winchester pub, still in Southwark Bridge Road, was probably the site of the first music hall. Not far from it was the Borough, or Raglan, in Union Street. The grandest of the Southwark music-halls was the South London Palace in London Road, near the Elephant & Castle, not just a hall behind a pub, but a specially built theatre that could hold up to 4,000 people. Famous 'old timers' who appeared here included Albert Chevalier and Marie Lloyd.

All the old theatres, music halls and other entertainments of North Southwark have gone, but it still has many pubs which, as you can see if you look up, above the ground floor, were built in Victorian or earlier times, for example the Crown and the Rising Sun in Blackfriars Road. Pubs with these names have been here since at least 1826. The sign of a modern pub, The Ring, reminds you that it is across the road from the scene of many famous fights.

Finding out more

1 Read the *Survey* Vol. XXII, p. 115-7 and 119-20 and Vol. XXV, p. 57-8.

2 The Local Studies Library has many playbills of the Surrey Theatre, South London Palace, etc.

3 Find plaques marking sites of the Rotunda and Surrey Chapel.

4 At the Cuming Museum see animals from the Leverian Museum, and model of South London Palace.

5 Study *Scenes from the Past,* Ser. 3, No. 1.

6 Read *Conquest, the story of a theatre family* by F. Fleetwood, Part III
and *'Neath the mask* by J. M. East p. 113-20.

Clink Street, 1974.

11. WAREHOUSES AND THE RIVER TRADE

For over a hundred years, until about 1970, the Southwark riverfront
was lined with tall warehouses like those which still overshadow part of
Clink Street. Goods were brought by red-sailed barges and by 'lighters',
propelled by wind, tide and oars, to be landed by cranes and stored in
these warehouses until taken to their destinations. The narrow riverside
streets were once crowded with traffic and men at work.

Ever since Roman times, the Thames had been a highway for trade.
During building work at Guy's Hospital, remains of a Roman ship were
found in what had once been a inlet of the Thames. The entry for
Southwark in Domesday Book mentions 'tolls on the riverbank' and 'the
tideway where ships are moored' which was probably St. Mary Overie's
Dock, the little inlet near Southwark Cathedral. Until a few years' ago,
the dock had a notice which read:

ST. MARY OVERIE'S DOCK
This dock is a Free Landing Place at which the Parishioners of St.
Saviour's Parish are entitled to Land Goods Free of Toll.

In the 19th century London and London's trade increased enormously.
Rennie's new London Bridge with wider arches made it possible for
barges to get up river and this was when Bankside became especially
busy and the great warehouses were built. Pickford's warehouses in
Clink Street, erected in 1864, with five stories and cellars, were originally
intended for storing flour, hops and seeds. When more space was
needed and there was no room for expansion on the riverside, new
warehouses were built on the south side of Clink Street, connected with
the old by iron bridges across the street. Further up river there are other
old warehouses at Stamford Wharf, Upper Ground. Above them rises
the Oxo Tower, a riverside landmark since it was erected in 1928.

When the warehouses were laden with goods and the river busy with
ships, many families lived around Bankside, near their work, for

example, the Harris family of Park Street who had been lightermen on the river for many generations. In his autobiography, *Under Oars,* Harry Harris describes his childhood, playing among the boats on the foreshore and learning to swim in the river. His father, knowing well the dangers of falling in or 'going overboard' was always on the look-out for tell-tale mud on young Harry's boots! The Bankside Regatta was an annual event with boat races and a band playing on a river barge. The family holiday was a trip by boat from Bankside to Yarmouth. Naturally when Harry grew up he became a Freeman of the Watermen and Lightermen's Company.

Every year since 1715 young Thames watermen have competed in a rowing race from London Bridge to Chelsea. The prize is 'Doggett's Coat and Badge'. The new pub by Blackfriars Bridge has used the badge as its sign. On it is a wild horse, the emblem of the Royal House of Hanover. The prize was first awarded by Thomas Doggett, an actor, for a race on the first anniversary of George I's accession to the throne.

Finding out more

1 Read *Under Oars* by Harry Harris, publ. Centerprise 1978.

2 Study illustrations in *Old Bankside* by G. Golden.

3 Study GLIAS Reports on *Pickford's Wharf, Clink Wharf and St. Mary Overie's, Rosing's and Stave Wharves.*

12. FACTORY CHIMNEYS

'An array of tall chimneys – each one – a guide post to some large manufacturing establishment beneath – here a brewery, there a sawmill, farther on a hat factory, a distillery, a vinegar factory and numerous others. Southwark is as distinguishable for its tall chimneys and clouds of smoke emitted by them, as London is for its church spires'.
From *Days in the Factories,* by G. Dodd, 1843

This was the view of Southwark from the City in the days of Queen Victoria. It was almost like the industrial towns of northern England. By 1871 industries, warehouses and railways had taken over so much land where earlier there had been houses that people were having to move out and the population had already begun to decline. Factories were built here because coal, iron and other heavy materials could be brought by river. The new bridges, roads and railways made it easy to transport the finished goods. The chimneys were necessary because the factories used steam power. In fact, the first James Watt steam-engine used to grind corn into flour was installed in the Albion Mills, near Blackfriars Bridge. It attracted many visitors until the mills were destroyed by fire in 1791.

In 1843 the largest factory chimney was that of Barclay Perkins' brewery in Park Street. Brewing was one of Southwark's oldest industries. Even in Chaucer's *Canterbury Tales* the Miller explained,

'And if the words get muddled in my tale
Just put it down to too much Southwark ale.'

In 1955 Barclay Perkins' amalgamated with that other great local brewery, Courage's of Bermondsey. This long history of brewing only came to an end in 1982 when Courage's finally closed both its local factories.

Some old Southwark factories were concerned with food, for example, Pott's Vinegar Works in Park Street, Epps' Steam Cocoa Mills in Hopton Street, and Stevenson and Howell's in Bear Lane, which produced flavourings for biscuits, ice creams etc.

Coal hole cover, Blackfriars Road
From *Coal Hole Rubbings*, by Lily Goddard,
Midas Books, 1979.

Many of the Southwark chimneys, however, belonged to engineering works and foundries. As you go about London and throughout the country look out for objects made in Southwark factories. In the pavements, for example in Blackfriars Road, you often see round, cast-iron, coal-hole covers, where the coalman used to shoot the coal down into the cellar below, in the days when everyone had coal fires. Many of the covers are patterned and inscribed, 'Hayward Brothers, Union Street, Borough'. The name, Haywards, is also seen on pavement glass which lets light into undergound cellars and basements. The firm was in Union Street from 1848 to 1976 and had a shop at the corner of Union Street and Blackfriars Road. A sign which is now in the Cuming Museum hung out above the shop door. Charles Dickens described it as 'the likeness of a golden dog licking a golden pot'.

The original waterworks for the fountains in Trafalgar Square were made in 1844 by another Southwark engineering firm, Easton and Amos of 'The Grove', now renamed Ewer Street. Issler's of Bear Lane specialised in artesian wells. Coles' Cranes was founded in 1879 by Henry Coles at his Steam Crane & Engineering Works in Sumner Street. Willcox's is one of the few big engineering firms still in north Southwark. Over buildings in Southwark Street to which they moved in 1880 you read in large letters 'Willcox's Tubes, Fittings and Valves' and 'Willcox's Flexible Hoses'.

One unique Southwark firm, Kirkaldy's Testing & Experimenting Works, 99 Southwark Street, has been made into a museum by the Industrial Buildings Preservation Trust. Over the entrance is David Kirkaldy's motto 'Facts, not opinions' and inside is the wonderful machine that he invented for testing the strength of building materials. It could put on as much as 300 tons of pressure and weighs 126 tons.

On Bankside one big chimney is still standing. It belongs to Bankside Power Station designed by Sir Giles Gilbert Scott and completed in 1963. For over a century and a half much of the light, heat and power for London came from Bankside. Long before electricity was in use, the Phoenix Gas Works, one of the earliest in London, occupied this site. Near it from 1883 to 1977 was a pumping station of the London Hydraulic Power Company which used the Thames to supply water power at a pressure of 700 pounds per square inch, to work lifts and cranes throughout London and even to raise Tower Bridge. Look out for the letters LHP set in roads around here. On 12th June 1891 the first public supply of electricity for the City of London was switched on from a small power station on Bankside.

Bankside Power Station ceased to generate electricity in 1981 but the regional headquarters of the Central Electricity Generating Board is still on Bankside.

Finding out more

1 Read *Days in the Factories* by G. Dodd, Chap. 2 and *A draught of contentment* by J. Pudney p. 43-80.

2 There are books or articles in the Local Studies Library on most firms – e.g. *Stevenson & Howell; a firm of flavour & fragrance; Years of reflection, the story of Haywards; Willcox's Centenary 1878-1978; Coles 100 years, the growth story of Europe's leading crane manufacturers.*

3 Read *Coalhole rubbings* by L. Goddard and do rubbings of coalhole covers.

4 Arrange a visit to Kirkaldy's Testing and Experimenting Works Museum.

5 See a beam engine by Easton & Amos, 1863, at the Living Steam Museum, Kew Bridge Road, Brentford.

13. THE FIRE BRIGADE

With warehouses storing inflammable goods and factories burning coal, fire was a constant danger in north Southwark. From 1878 to 1937 the headquarters of the London Fire Brigade was in Southwark Bridge Road. As the letters over the entrance to the Fire Station tell you, it was built for the M.F.B. (Metropolitan Fire Brigade) in 1878, by the M.B.W. (Metropolitan Board of Works – forerunner of the London County Council and the G.L.C.). A fireman at the station in the early years described what happened when there was a fire, 'Horses are harnessed in a trice, doors flung back – a wild ringing of bells, shouts and clatter of hooves on cobbles, and out thunders the fire engine'.

Captain Shaw, who was Chief Officer of the Fire Brigade until 1891, built up at Southwark Bridge Road a fire service that was the admiration of all and many visitors came to see the weekly drills and rescues from the practice tower. On stage they sang –

> 'O Captain Shaw
> Could thy Brigade
> With cold cascade
> Quench my great love, I wonder'

from *Iolanthe* by Gilbert & Sullivan.

Captain Shaw lived at Winchester House, the fine mansion next door to the fire station, now used as the Fire Brigade Recruiting and Training Centre and Museum. You can still see his look-out tower. Part of Winchester House is about two hundred years old and was built as a workhouse for St. Saviour's Parish. It was later used as a factory for hat-making, one of Southwark's old industries.

Ayres Street is named after the young heroine of one of Southwark's fires. In 1885, when fire broke out at an oil-merchant's in Union Street, Alice Ayres, nursemaid to the family who lived over the shop, threw three children down to safety before she herself fell from the blazing building and died.

Finding out more

1 Read *London's Fire Brigade* by W. E. Jackson, Chap. 6-10 and *London's noble fire brigades* 1833-1914 by S. Holloway, Chaps. 6 & 7.

2 Arrange a visit to the Fire Brigade Museum, Southwark Bridge Road. (Open by appointment only).

14. HOMES, OLD AND NEW

About 6,600 people now live in Cathedral Ward, the part of Southwark which includes Bankside and Blackfriars Road. If you are one of them you may be among the first residents of a new estate, or your home may be a house where people have lived and children have grown up for over 200 years.

The oldest houses are Nos. 49-52 Bankside. They help you to imagine this riverside street as it was before the bridges, factories and warehouses were built when many people must have had similar pleasant houses here. No. 49, Cardinal's Wharf, even has a plaque claiming that 'Christopher Wren lived here'. Though there is no evidence for this it certainly has a good view of St. Paul's. (More probably Wren watched the progress of his cathedral from a house near the Falcon Inn, long since demolished.) The coat of arms on Cardinal's Wharf is modern, belonging to the Munthe family, present owners of the house. The rainwater pipe, inscribed 1712, is a clue to the date of Nos. 50-52 Bankside. These houses have been restored as the Provost's Lodgings for the Provost of Southwark Cathedral. The cathedral coat of arms hangs outside.

Not far away, hemmed in by industrial buildings and office blocks you find Hopton's Almshouses in Hopton Street. These delightful cottages round a courtyard garden have provided homes for old people ever since they were built in 1752 under the will of Charles Hopton. A small house, 61 Hopton Street, is even older, dating from about 1703.

These old houses were here when Dr. Samuel Johnson, author of a famous dictionary and many books, and a brilliant conversationalist, used to come over to Southwark to visit his friends Mr. and Mrs. Thrale. Henry Thrale, M.P. for Southwark, owned the brewery which later became Barclay Perkins. At their house in Park Street, his wife Hester entertained many famous writers and artists, including Oliver Goldsmith, who had earlier practised as a physician on Bankside, and Sir Joshua Reynolds, first President of the Royal Academy. The Anchor pub, also once owned by Henry Thrale, has been restored to look just as though you were back in the 18th century, with many reminders of Dr. Johnson and his biographer, James Boswell. There is a copy of her portrait by Reynolds in what has been named 'Mrs. Thrale's bar'.

The Anchor and the old houses of Bankside and Hopton Street are now 'Listed Buildings'. Also on the *List of buildings of special architectural or historic interest* are many fine Georgian houses built soon after the new roads were laid out, such as Nos. 75 – 86 Blackfriars Road and 63 – 68 St. George's Road. Notice the beautiful doorways and ironwork balconies. Some still have old boot-scrapers at the foot of well-worn steps. Three sides of West Square, a conservation area, look almost exactly as they did when built about 1794. In Glasshill Street are the 'Drapers Almshouses, rebuilt AD 1820', now occupied as private houses, and in Gladstone Street, the elegant Albert Terrace of 1849.

Some old houses are used for special purposes. Before World War II, Nelson Square was surrounded by Georgian houses. The only ones left belong to the Blackfriars Settlement which carries on the good community work begun here in 1891 by the Women's University Settlement. No. 74 Blackfriars Road is a builder's shop. Anchor Terrace, Nos. 1-15 Southwark Bridge Road, built 1834, was the headquarters of Barclay Perkins, and now of Courage's. It has over it the Royal Coat of Arms, 'By authority of his Majesty William IV'.

In early Victorian times, the population of north Southwark increased enormously. The peak was in 1861 when nearly 89,000 people lived in the three parishes of St. Saviour, Christ Church and St. George the Martyr. Poor people lived in overcrowded conditions in small back streets between Blackfriars Road and Borough High Street. Often they were close to high factory walls, which shut out light and air and they endured continual noise, vibration, smoke and fumes, from factories and railways. According to an article in the magazine of St. Alphege's Church, Lancaster Street, 'all disagreeable smelling trades were carried on in the neighbourhood, haddock smokers, bone-boilers, horse slaughterers,' and 'half-washed clothes dangled from clothes lines stretched across the street'. There are still some of these small streets, for example, Copperfield Street, Sawyer Street and Pepper Street. They are not crowded now and there is no noise or smoke. They now have pleasant cottage-type houses built in 1894 by the Church Commissions under the influence of that great housing reformer Octavia Hill. As you walk through these streets you can sense the good side of the old way of life. They are peaceful, almost traffic-free, and have the friendly feeling of a little community.

In her book *Old Bankside* Grace Golden recalled 'the narrow alleys opening on to Bankside – like black caves inviting me to explore them'. This is another area where living conditions were bad, but it seems sad that instead of being improved most of these alleys totally disappeared in 1929 beneath Bankside Power Station. The old street pattern and names which went back to Shakespeare's day – Love Lane, Moss Alley, Unicorn Alley, White Hind Alley – have all been forgotten.

Today many people live in blocks of flats, the oldest being Cromwell Buildings, Redcross Way, built by the Improved Industrial Dwellings Company in 1864. There are many belonging to the Peabody Trust, Peabody Square, Blackfriars Road, built in 1872, is a good example. Other flats were built by the L.C.C. in its early years. Over the entrances to Hunter, Murray and Gardiner Houses in King James Street, off Borough Road, there is Victoria type decoration and the date 1899. Since the 16th century the City of London has owned much land in Southwark. It forms part of the Bridgehouse Estates which provide income to maintain the four City bridges, London, Southwark, Blackfriars and Tower Bridge. Look out for the Bridge House Mark on flats built on this land, for example on Pakeman House, Pocock Street.

Bridge House Mark.

After the bombing of World War II there was much rebuilding and also redevelopment to improve conditions. Council flats replaced the bombed Georgian houses of Nelson Square, names being taken from local history, for example, Rowland Hill House, and Vaughan House after a leading family in old Christ Church parish. The more recent Council estate in Nicholson Street, on the other hand, provides what most families want, small houses with gardens. Flats in Edward Edwards House, Nicholson Street, are for elderly ladies. They were built by a charity founded by Edward Edwards of Christ Church parish in 1717. One of the latest Southwark Council developments is Falcon Point. Its residents have a view over the Thames such as few can have enjoyed for centuries.

Finding out more

1 Look at any 'Listed Buildings' near your home or school. Should others be added to the list?

2 Read *Survey* Vol. XXII, p. 59-63, p. 78-80, p. 88-9, p. 111-4, p. 117-8 and p. 129-132, and Vol. XXV p. 60-4.

3 Read *Inns of old Southwark* by W. Rendle, p. 353-7.

4 Read *Old Bankside* by G. Golden, preface, p. 53-62 and p. 171-2.

5 Look up your street in old *Ordnance Survey maps, Directories,* and *Census returns* (on microfilm), at the Local Studies Library.

6 For architectural detail study *The Buildings of England, London 2, South,* p. 555-592.

7 Look out for any marks or plaques on buildings. Who put them there and what do they mean?

15. CHURCHES AND SCHOOLS

There cannot be many neighbourhoods like north Southwark which have two cathedrals, the old church which is now the Anglican Southwark Cathedral and St. George's, the Roman Catholic Cathedral, in St. George's Road.

St. George's was built in 1848 thanks to the efforts of a priest named Thomas Doyle. Earlier Catholics had worshipped in a small chapel in London Road, but a large church was needed when many Irish people came to work in South London. The great Victorian architect, A. W. N. Pugin designed the church in the gothic style, like churches of the Middle Ages. It became a cathedral with a bishop in 1850. Almost destroyed in World War II, St. George's was rebuilt using what was left of Pugin's building and adding a clerestory. Inside it is wonderfully light and peaceful. Looking up you see on the painted timber roof symbols of the Bible story, from the sun, moon and stars of the Creation to the kings' crowns and shepherds' crooks of Christmas. One little chapel is in

St. George's Roman Catholic Cathedral.

memory of Edward Petre, a benefactor of the cathedral. Another is dedicated to St. Peter and the English Martyrs, many of whom were imprisoned in the Clink or the old prisons of Borough High Street. In 1982 Pope John Paul II celebrated mass in St. George's for over 3,000 sick people. Next door is Archbishop Amigo Jubilee Hall named after the priest who was Bishop and then Archbishop of Southwark from 1904 to 1949.

Christ Church, Blackfriars Road is an interesting church of a very different kind. It replaces the old Christ Church which was destroyed in World War II. In the garden behind it you can see the outline of the cross which fell in flames on 17th April 1941 scorching the grass. The new church, opened in 1960, is the headquarters of the South London Industrial Mission which aims to bring the Christian message to places where people work and also to help the unemployed. Go into the church to see the beautiful stained glass windows with pictures, not of ancient saints, but of Southwark workers, for example, the boatman on the river, the printer with his press, the brewer with bags of hops, the engineer with machinery and even the secretary in her office and the cleaning lady. The church garden used to be the burial ground. One gravestone reads, 'To the memory of John Lloyd, Millwright and Engineer who died 1836', an older link with local industry. John Marshall Hall is named after the man who left money over three hundred years ago for the founding of the first Christ Church and for other good purposes. He lived in Newcomen Street where the offices of the John Marshall Charity are still to be found.

The oldest chapel for Welsh people living in London was in Southwark. In 1873 its members moved to the big Welsh Church in Southwark Bridge Road. Other churches still in use include the Roman Catholic Church of the Most Precious Blood in O'Meara Street, built in 1892. Some churches are now no more. The ruins standing in the little public garden in Copperfield Street are all that is left of All Hallows, bombed in World War II. The magnificent doric arch, or portico, in Stamford Street was once the entrance to a Unitarian Chapel, built in 1821.

The oldest schools were church schools. St. Saviour's Parish School was founded over three hundred years ago. St. Jude's Church has closed but children are still educated at St. Jude's School as they have been since the 1860s. St. George's Roman Catholic Schools first opened in 1854. Two Sisters of Notre Dame, nuns from Namur in Belgium, who came to Southwark in 1855, started the school which became Notre Dame High School for Girls.

The London Nautical School, for boys who hope to join the Royal Navy or Merchant Navy, started in Rotherhithe but now occupies fine buildings in Stamford Street erected in 1803, originally as a school for Irish children.

After 1870 many schools were built by the London School Board and later by the L.C.C., for example the school in West Square. On the outside you read, 'St. George's Road School 1884'. It has been renamed the Charlotte Sharman School after a lady who founded an orphanage in West Square. In 1900 over three hundred little girls were living in 'Miss

Sharman's Homes', the buildings which are now All Saints Hospital, Austral Street. Friars School opened in 1916. Friar Street was the old name for Webber Street.

You do not have far to go for higher education in north Southwark. The Polytechnic of the South Bank, one of the largest colleges for science, technology and other subjects in England, began here as the 'Borough Poly' in 1892. In its early years it had classes for poor boys and girls who otherwise had no chance of further education after they left 'board school' at thirteen. As well as its old buildings in Borough Road it has huge modern buildings in London Road. Not far away are Southwark College for Further Education and Morley College, on the borders of Southwark and Lambeth.

Borough Road Library opened in 1899 as the library for St. George the Martyr parish. As you go in look up at the terra-cotta relief above the entrance showing St. George fighting the dragon.

Finding out more

1 Read *Survey,* Vol. XXV, Chap. 8 and Vol. XXII, Chaps. 19 and 23.

2 Read *Buildings of England; London 2: South* p. 572-8.

3 Read *The Great Link; a history of St. George's Cathedral* by B. Bogan.

4 Read *Charlotte Sharman* by M. Williams.

5 Read *A history of Borough Road College* by G. F. Bartle, and *Borough Polytechnic 1892-1969* by F. G. Evans.

16. A NEW CHAPTER

The cloud-capped towers, the gorgeous palaces,
The solemn temples, the great globe itself,
Yea, all which it inherit shall dissolve.
                              Shakespeare *The Tempest*

Over the centuries, north Southwark has seen many changes. 'The Great Globe' itself was short-lived, though it brought lasting fame to Bankside. Some of the most rapid changes have been during the lifetime of older people. Wartime destruction and, later, closure of factories and warehouses have made way for totally new developments. As part of central London, Bankside has always shared in the life of the capital, providing first for its entertainment and later for its trade and industry. Now, newly cleared sites give space for office blocks. In Southwark Street and Sumner Street big government departments replaced small houses and shops destroyed in World War II. Then came Lloyd's Computer Centre east of Blackfriars Bridge and the King's Reach development of offices and flats west of it.

For lovers of history it has been a sad time. Old familiar sights seem to vanish overnight. Rose Alley, which led to the Rose Theatre, is blocked by offices. Horseshoe Alley, which led to the Globe, has disappeared. The special enclosed character of Clink Street and St. Mary Overie Dock has been partly lost. For residents of north Southwark, the changes have been more devastating. Warehouses closing and factories moving out has led to loss of jobs. The new offices cannot use their skills. New developments do not always include housing or amenities for local people. Many, therefore, have left to find jobs or homes. This has meant that shops have closed for lack of customers and schools for lack of children, all making things worse for those who remain.

It has never been very easy for local people to get together to improve matters. The district is divided by main roads. Before 1900 it was part of three civil parishes, St. Saviour's, Christ Church and St. George the Martyr, each with its own local government. Later it was part of the Metropolitan Borough of Southwark and since 1965 of the large London Borough of Southwark. Its problems it probably shares more with its neighbours in north Lambeth.

But now little groups are getting together to say what they would like for their own localities. The North Southark Community Development Group supports their efforts. Local residents already see some signs of hope for them. The site of Courage's, bought by the G.L.C., is intended for housing and industry. There is a new Bankside Industrial Centre in Bear Lane. There are new open spaces, such as Grotto Place, where there had been derelict sites. Since Sainsbury's food factory in Stamford Street closed in 1973 a local self-help project has converted their staff canteen into the Colombo Street Sports and Community Centre. The old Southwark Bridge Road Library built in 1894 is now the Borough Community Centre. SE1, a newspaper published in Meymott Street, keeps people informed of what is going on.

It is time perhaps to return to Bankside itself, where the history of this neighbourhood began. You find after years of decline it is springing to new life. Set out then from King's Reach; space-age architecture this seems indeed, especially when you look up at its 30 storey tower block piercing the sky. Making your way towards London Bridge you come first to Bankside Reach, a large traffic-free open space with new paving, lawns and shrubs, where local people, Londoners and tourists can sit out and enjoy the sunshine and the river view, no longer hidden behind industrial buildings. The new Founder's Arms, replacing an older pub of that name, is near the site of an iron foundry which prepared the railings for Christopher Wren's St. Paul's. Exhibitions open to the public are presented at the Bankside Gallery, headquarters of the Royal Society of Painters in Water Colours and the Royal Society of Painter-Etchers and Engravers.

Beyond the Power Station are links with the past, Nos. 49 and 50-52 Bankside, and between them Cardinal Cap Alley, the one Bankside alley which, amazingly, has survived unaltered in shape since the 16th century. Then you come to the Anchor, much rebuilt and extended since the last war, but still 18th century in appearance. In Clink Street are some Victorian warehouses restored for new uses, and the rose window and newly uncovered foundations of Winchester Palace.

At Southwark Cathedral there is an exciting mixture of old and new. Montague Close, site of a Roman road, medieval priory, 17th and 18th century industries and 19th century warehouses, is now an open courtyard overlooking the river. The ancient Cathedral, no longer hemmed in by other buildings, is adding an extension for service to the community. On the west of the courtyard is Minerva House, flats and bank offices, designed to fit in well with its surroundings. On the east is Hibernia Chambers built in 1850, now restored as the Glaziers' Company Hall, near the site of early Southwark glassworks. Outside the new Mudlark pub, the history of London Bridge is inscribed in words and pictures on stones saved from Rennie's Bridge.

Mounting to the bridge itself, you look again up river and see that a new chapter in Bankside's long history is about to begin.

Finding out more

1 Do walks suggested in *The Cathedral Ward Urban Study* and *Walk Around Historic Southwark*. Both are L.B. Southwark publs.

2 Study the *North Southwark Plan* and any other redevelopment plans.

LONDON BOROUGH OF SOUTHWARK NEIGHBOURHOOD HISTORIES,
already published:

1 The Story of Camberwell.

2 The Story of Dulwich.

3 The Story of Peckham.

4 The Story of Walworth.

5 The Story of Bermondsey.

6 The Story of Rotherhithe.

7 The Story of 'The Borough'.

This book was produced by members of the staff of the London Borough of Southwark Libraries Department.

Text by Mary Boast.

Illustrated by David A. Burch.

Illustrations are drawings from prints and photographs in the Local Studies Library.

Published by the Council of the London Borough of Southwark, 1985.

Printed in England by Frowde and Co., (Printers) Ltd., Orpheus Street, Camberwell Green, London SE5.